Lit from Within

Praise for Annette Childs and *"Will You Dance?"*

A Book for the Journey... a Story for the Soul

This debut work by Annette Childs received critical acclaim, and was named **Gift Book of the Year** and **New Age Book of the Year** in 2002

"Annette Childs has done the world a service by writing this book . . . "
Raymond A. Moody, Jr., MD, PhD, Bestselling author of *Life After Life*

"Upon meeting Annette some years back, I was immediately overcome with the sense that this woman had a message to share with the world. ***Will You Dance?*** *speaks to the wisest part within each of us, and this book will be a cherished companion for anyone traversing the dark night of the soul."* **Andy Lakey**
Author of *Art, Angels and Miracles*

"What a beautiful, beautiful gift is being given to all through the publication of this book! A beam to show the reasons why and wherefore. This is a book for Little Ones and Old Ones and the heart in all of us who long to know . . . "
Kanta Masters, President, Source Seminars

*"****Will You Dance?*** *is a symbolic story that defines the life experiences of most of us at one time or another. This is a highly recommended and enjoyable read, written in an almost poetic style."* **Harold McFarland**
Midwest Book Review
Amazon.com Top 50 Reviewer

Praise for **Annette Childs and** *"Halfway Across the River"*

Messages of Hope from the Other Side

Halfway Across the River won the 2008 **Benjamin Franklin Gold Medal** for **Best New Age Title** and was the 2009 recipient of the **Silver Nautilus Award**.

"Annette Childs is a warm, bright, and accomplished psychotherapist who has spent the bulk of her career working with the dying and the bereaved; thus her writing comes from a heartfelt understanding of the struggles that eventually plague us all."
Raymond A. Moody, Jr., MD, PhD, Bestselling author of *Life After Life*

*"Annette Childs, artist of metaphors, has written another touching and meaningful book. **Halfway Across the River** offers lessons about life, death, grief, and transcendence. Although educational and enlightening, it is terrifically entertaining and reader friendly."* **Dianne Arcangel**
Author of *Afterlife Encounters* **and** *Life After Loss*

"For those of us who have spent our lives in the care of the dying, one of the greatest rewards come from those who share stories of moments that transcend the ordinary experiences of life. These moments arrive in the form of 'messages' from across the veil. Those who have the gift of recognizing these messages are charged with a great responsibility in sharing them with the rest of us. Dr. Annette Childs is one of these extraordinary individuals. In *Halfway Across the River*, she has captured these stories with incredible grace, wisdom and compassion. Her latest book provides a message of hope for any who question, "Is this all there is?" Her stories help others to suspend their disbelief and provide hope for anyone who has experienced a loss."

Deb Girard, RN
Founder, Circle of Life Hospice

"Upon meeting Annette some years back, I was immediately overcome with the sense that this woman had a message to share with the world ..."

Andy Lakey
Author of *Art, Angels and Miracles*

"Annette Childs, PhD, has been blessed with a natural ability to connect with invisible energies, enabling her to assist the dying and their loved ones as they cope with the process of transition. With humor and poignant honesty she has compiled dramatic examples of communication between this reality and the other side that will touch the heart of all who read it. ***Halfway Across the River*** is a beautiful, well written inspirational journey of peacefulness and love. This book will elicit spontaneous tears of joy, as fear is magically transmuted to a deep and reassuring understanding of the continuum that is life and death."

Jeffrey D. Millman, MD
Author of *A Giant Leap of Faith*

Lit From Within

© Copyright 2009 by Annette Childs, Ph.D.

ALL RIGHTS RESERVED

~First Printing~

2010

ISBN 0-9718902-7-7

Library of Congress Control Number: 2009930168

Illustrations by Ann Rothan

Back Cover Photo: Kelly Wheeler

Dedication Photo: Michael Imus

Book Design: Paul Cirac, White Sage Studios, Virginia City, NV

Signed copies of
Dr. Childs' other books

"Halfway Across the River"
and
"Will You Dance?"

are available

If you would like more information or
to place an order please visit our website

www.onecandle.net

or call
The Wandering Feather Press
at
1-775-853-4142

Lit from Within

~A book for the Evolving Soul~

Annette Childs, Ph.D.
Illustrated by Ann Rothan

THE
Wandering
Feather
PRESS

4790 Caughlin Pkwy, #103
Reno, Nevada 89519
www.onecandle.net

Acknowledgements

*T*his book was released into the world as gently as one would launch a paper boat onto the sea, with a hopeful nudge and a prayer behind it. In years past I could not have come from such a place of faith, but life has softened me. For a while now the universe has held me in strong, yet gentle hands. My restless yearning to push forward has been tempered with a quiet acceptance that the journey through life ebbs and flows in different ways for each of us.

Faith in that journey has been my gift, yet this gift has been augmented greatly with the support of amazing people who keep me balanced and sturdy on my path.

To those who helped bring this book to life:

*A*nn Rothan, for your grace, your vision, and the elegance that your artwork brings to these words; Pam Bickell, my word surgeon, thank you for the nips and tucks; your elation at my journey never fails to fill my sails with wind…thank you; Paul Cirac, the 'one man band' who builds my books sturdy and strong: where else but at White Sage Studios can one disappear into the Comstock and emerge a few hours later with a book ready to deliver to the world?

To my readers, students, and clients, who continually return to drink the nectar of my words: Thank you for your faith in me and for allowing me to do what I love and call it work.

To my inner circle, thank you:

My parents, Bill and Grace: You continually expand your vision to meet me where I am, and you elongate it as well, to help me capture who I am becoming. I know that my philosophies and life path have stretched you both. Thank you for loving me enough to always let me run with the gifts that God has given me.

My three children: You embody every good quality a mother could hope for in her offspring. Sutter, so gentle and wise; Delaney, so beautiful and strong; and Ajay, so wild and determined. You each teach me, inspire me and push me to forge a wider path forward so that your way might someday be made easier, too.

To my husband Brian: I love you. This phrase in some ways seems too small, but I mean it in every simple and profound way that the words can be interpreted. The day you came into my world, everything changed. The storms became bearable, the swell of gratitude became constant, and I learned finally what it was to live in the shelter of a life held secure by faith, love, and a shared journey forward. Today, tomorrow, always, and in all ways, I love you.

And finally, to The Ones Who Speak. You are nameless and formless, with no beginning and no end. Yet when you find me and move through me, I am both captured and free, awash in a sea of words that I somehow get to call mine. Thank you for the gift of these words…may this book be a worthy vessel to carry them into the world.

A Note to the Reader...

This is a book that poured itself through me in the last days of my pregnancy with my third child. The early words of this story had lived within me for years, as I waited patiently for life to unfold and bring to me the third child I had always hoped to have. Quite literally in the last hours of that pregnancy, the story completed itself and made its way into this world along with my child. So what you will read is raw, a lexis that has not been altered by an editor or anyone else who might change the alchemy of the words that formed in a torrent and carried me along with them.

At the time I thought of these words as a gift from a high being who I believed would accompany my child into his incarnation.

I could feel this presence as it stood next to me, forming complete sentences much faster than my fingers could type. Indeed, as new life kicked in my belly, this story coursed through me with a life of its own. It was complete except for the final pages and a title... but the torrent of words stopped and I sat in silence wondering, "What now?"

The very next day a woman walked into my home and as soon as she took my hand in hers and said hello, I again felt that same great being of light beside me, forming words in my mind. This woman, Eileen, was

92-years-old and exuded the quiet elegance that comes with having traveled gracefully upon the path one is given. Eileen was lit from within in a way that took my breath away. She shone with a luminosity that wrapped around her like a veil. It did not hide her age, but let it fall around her in great waves of beauty. I knew immediately that this story was not just my child's, but Eileen's story too—indeed, a story that belongs to each of us. It is the story of the beginning of life, and follows us through to journey's end.

So dear reader, these words are yours. This book is simply a sacred container for an ancient flame that belongs to us all. With each reading of it, may one more candle burn brightly against the darkness of our unknowing. And if this story touches you deeply, pass its flame to one whose journey has grown dark … for our own flame is never diminished by lighting the path of another.

As you take this book into your hands, know that just as I had a great being beside me as I wrote these words, you too have a great being of your own beside you as you read them. Your Guardian of the light has waited patiently to sing you awake. Read now the story of your own becoming. Gently awaken from the sleepy drone of mediocrity, and know that your journey is sacred, and that this life you were given is a candle, meant to bring light to the world.

This book is dedicated to Ajay and Eileen...
one the Alpha,
moist with the dew of new life;
the other the Omega,
carved in beauty by the hands of time.

Together,
you made these words whole.

The Shining One sat quietly in his chair,
watching small lights
flicker in the distance.
Deep in thought, he fingered his
long gray beard as he gently held the
gaze of those who stood before him.

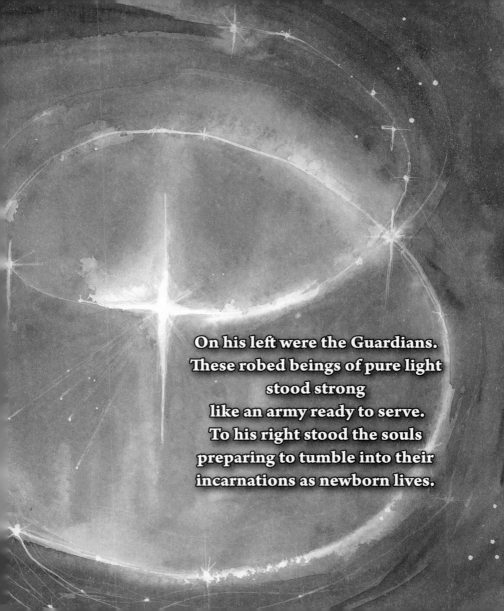

On his left were the Guardians.
These robed beings of pure light
stood strong
like an army ready to serve.
To his right stood the souls
preparing to tumble into their
incarnations as newborn lives.

**Two-by-two
they stepped forward,
and one-by-one
they took their vows.**

To the Guardians, the Shining One spoke
in a tone that was both even and kind.
The question was always the same.
"Do you commit your light
to the service of this soul?"

And to the souls
he asked simply,
"Do you accept
the weight of illusion
that will soon bear down upon you?"

The
sacred
pact
in place,
the
universe
unfolds…

Like a spindle of golden
thread unleashed,
the souls fall
miles and lifetimes
into their incarnations,
their Guardians
following
behind
in trails of light.

Together they will spend their days . . .
the Guardians
working tirelessly
to sing the souls awake,
and the souls
struggling to peek beyond
their own
heavy cloaks of forgetting.

And so it was
on the day of your becoming
that the Shining One sent us forth . . .
You as a soul,
and I,
as your Guardian of the light.

With the cloak of forgetting fastened
firmly about you,
blithely you
stepped
into your incarnation.
Certain were you
that you would
remember your lineage
as a child of God.

Yet almost immediately,
misperception
blanketed you
like a tightly wound cocoon.
As you grew
and the tempo of your life
became
stronger,
the tenor
of your soul grew quiet.

As the cloak
of forgetting
tightened around
you,
your
sleepy
eyes closed to truth.

Today, I rouse you gently
with the
chanting of your soul's own song.
Sit quietly now as I tell you
the story of
your becoming.
Let my words echo gently through your
being, awakening a sacred memory
that has always been within you.

Remember, my child, you chose
this lifetime for all of the joys
and sorrows it contained.

You knowingly took this journey
for both the gifts
and the struggles.

Indeed,
although you may not
remember,
it was with an open heart
and a hopeful soul
that you embarked
upon
the path
you now walk.

Not a moment
of this life
has been in error.
Not one tear
has
been
in vain.

Each face
that you have caressed,
you've held a thousand times before.
Each name
you have cursed
has been that
of both your keeper
and your slave.

Every
moment
of darkness
and
each moment
of light:

They are
all carefully
chosen
threads
in the tapestry
of your days.

Your destiny
was formed long ago,
and the journey of this lifetime
is one
that your soul has taken
with the hope
that you will awaken.

Whether this day
finds you dewy
with youth,
or gnarled by age,
this moment is yours.

Open your
sleepy eyes now
and remember,
as I rouse
your ears
to the melody
of truth.

May this
remembering
of your soul's
own story
ignite the sacred flame
of truth within you,
so that wherever your journey may lead you
you will always be
lit from within.

Your
Story

It was with fingers
laced in gold
that a soft dark space
was carved in the
belly,
a sacred spot where the
journey called life first begins.

It was here,
as you lay gently cradled
in the warm and calm waters of the womb,
you first began to hear the call
of your own sacred name.

For just as your frame
was forming,
so did form the invisible.
And just as your cells
divided,
so too
did you divide yourself
from all destinies
other than your own.

On the day of your birth
as you emerged
in this world,
I placed my hands
upon the crown of
your tiny head.

As I looked down upon you,
at the tender
place where I could see
your heart beating,
I watched
and I listened
as your heart beat
to the rhythm
of your soul's own song.

And it was in the place
you call the
soft spot,
the one tiny place where the
structures of your body
had not yet
grown together,
that I took the breath
of becoming deep within me, and gently
I blew a sacred flame against the
tiny wick of your newborn life.

Your small body shuddered
as your destiny
fell softly upon you
and the light that was
your true essence
began its
steady glow.

From the day
you arrived
seeing life
through the misty eyes
of a newborn
it was I
who sang your soul awake.

As your mother cradled
you in her arms,
I began to whisper gently to you,
reminding you that this life
you were given was a candle
meant to
bring light to the world.

These words were long ago
etched in the deepest
part of your being.
They have, until today,
lay quiet like a seed within you,
waiting
for life to pull them forth
from
the fertile soil of your being.

Arriving new to this life,
you were buoyant
like
foam upon a wave . . .
kept pliant by your
soul's own tenderness.

Yet,
as you grew,
the weight of illusion
pressed down
upon you,

**beckoning you
to forget
your lineage
as a child of God.**

Today
I call out to you
with a gentle reminder
to let go the chains of forgetting
so that your life
can keep time
with the peaceful
cadence of your soul.

For you are meant
to dance to the music
in your heart,
and whether that melody
be somber or full of bliss,
the music within . . .
it belongs to only you.

On the shore
before you,
you will
undoubtedly
meet both joy and happiness.

Remember
that although
they seem to
travel arm in arm,
in truth
they inhabit
two
different worlds.

Happiness lives in the
moment . . .
always within your reach,
yet
she will roll in
and fade away
like the tides.

Joy stands on a distant shore
that you must
stretch yourself to reach . . .
but joy once
experienced
leaves an indelible
mark upon
your spirit,
one that will live inside you forever.

So welcome both
joy and happiness,
but choose
between
them
with care.

And no matter
how carefully you step,
in your life
there will be
broken places,
with edges
sharp and jagged.

Although these rough
edges
may cause
you to bleed,
do not
curse the breaking.

For within the breaking
resides
the healing,

and you will not
find one
without the other.

On the days
when you find yourself lost,
call to me.
I will blow gently upon the embers
of your inner flame
and in that moment your
darkness will recede
and your vision will be clear.

What was hazy
will become pristine
and as you see life
though new eyes,
you will behold miracles
in both the mundane
and the profound
moments that life offers you.

For miracles are
your
birthright,
but they
can be seen
only with
the eyes
of the soul.

When the roar
of loneliness
fills the soft
places within you,
turn your ears to the
whisperings of the universe.

There
you will hear my voice
imploring you
not to stay in the
chrysalis of your misperceptions,
but instead
to break through the shell
of illusion and emerge with the wings
of truth fastened firmly to your back.

As you
seek answers
to the quandaries of life,
allow both innocence and wisdom
to guide you.

**Although their tones
will be different,
they each
bear the fruit of knowing.**

The voice of innocence
will be subtle
like a compass pointing north,
leading you
to the things that
are true and whole within you.

The voice of wisdom
is deep and resonant.
It will shake you to your core.
Follow wisdom's council, for
although his ways are hard and steep,
in doing so, you will always find yourself
on the pathway to right living.

May you, sweet child,
be strong
enough to teach,
and may you
be humble
enough to learn.

And on your journey
may you be moved
forward
not just by the boisterous
call of glory,
but also
by the simple
and
tender
moments of your life.

When only unknown pathways lay
before you,
allow the voice of hope to
incubate within you, however small
and quiet
this voice may seem…

For hope has an echo that is easily
carried on the wind
and will go out
like a call
to the universe
beckoning all that
you seek to move one step closer to you.

And love,
she will introduce herself
to you only after she has already
made her home deep within you.

And, like a long awaited guest who
once arrived never leaves,
she will both
deplete
and
fulfill you.

**Her mystery
will draw you in
as quickly
as her fickleness
will cast you away...**

**Do not
be stymied
by her ways.**

Instead
let your heart
remain open
like a
window to the stars . . .

For
it is in loving
and being loved
that
you will find completion.

May your dreams
run free
like wild horses,
moving with abandon
upon
the canvas of your life.

And though youthful folly
my propel you,
may caution
sit quietly beside you like a good and faithful dog,
offering you
companionship
when life demands from you great stillness.

May laughter
unfurl
itself from deep within you,
like a
sail that
has caught its wind.

And as you flow
onward,
may equanimity
be the
ballast
that keeps
your journey
even and safe.

There will be times
when your laughter
will cease and you will be pulled from
the shores of contentment
by the ebb and flow
of sadness.

Do not resist
these currents;
instead
let them carry you out to
waters
that are both
deep and dark.

For the calm and quiet waters of sorrow
offer
the undistorted mirror
that is held
only by the hand of truth,
and it is here
that you will see your
own reflection most clearly.

Look
deeply upon these waters and
let
your
sorrow teach you.
Soon
you will find yourself
returned
to a safe harbor.

When the cool winds
of change bring a chill to
your core,
you will be tempted
to blanket yourself
with the familiar—rather than step into the storm.

It is then
that I will swaddle
you in kindness
and turn
your face
to the wind.

For although
the winds of change may sting you,
they will also
release you from
the complacency
that builds
walls instead of bridges.

There will be times
when the landscape
of your life
will be arid,
when your hopes
and dreams seem
dry like November's leaves.

It is at these times
you may find yourself
traveling
down the dusty road of regret.

Do not waste your vision
looking back
upon your missteps,
for behind you
exists neither
chance nor opportunity.

**Instead fix
your gaze
upon the horizon
before you.**

There you will see,
soft like
a sunrise,
my light rising to greet you.
Follow me
like a well worn path;
my trail
of light
will lead you home.

And anger,
anger will find you.

One day
you will round a corner
in your life
and there it will be . . .
untenable, holding an indignant posture.

Anger
will applaud
your righteousness
and sprinkle embers of contempt
upon
the sacred flame
that burns within you.

When anger's flame
has seared you,
I will
bring to you
the cool rains
of temperance.

It is then
that you will learn
that anger's fire
is
not akin
to your
own sacred flame,

but instead
a blaze that will
consume your
very self,
lest you learn
to quell its flames.

And when
the gnarled hands
of betrayal
touch the
soft clay that is your world,

you will
be tempted to
become
brittle and unyielding
to the beauty of this life.

Do not accept
the shackles of bitterness
that
betrayal offers,
for they are much too heavy
for the gentle rhythm of your ways.

**Instead
take the hand of forgiveness
that is always
demurely offered.**

She will step
from the shadows
and
quietly
lead you to wade in
the waters of tolerance.

To your surprise
you will find the current is gentle
and that tolerance
is not an anchor that binds
but instead
a vessel that provides safe passage.

**May you not
be lulled
to sleep by contentment,**

Lest you grow unable
to hear the voice of
gratitude
that lays quiet like a blanket
against your skin
on a cold winter's night.

**May you be
vigilant
and always
keep gratitude
awake in your heart . . .**

For gratitude
will lead you homeward
and
always return
you to
a place of love.

And when your time
in this world has been
long
and
you feel your days beginning
to fade,

May
you be filled
with the quiet
grace

that
follows
a
life
well
lived.

And may that sacred flame
with which
you were anointed
on the day of your
birth
burn brightly within you

**Warming you gently
with the knowing
that the journey
can never grow dark**

for one
who is
lit from within.

About the Author

Dr. Annette Childs holds a PhD in psychology and maintains a private practice assisting individuals and families to grow through painful transitions. As a researcher, she has extensively studied the mystical experiences that accompany the dying process, and she has also contributed original research to the field of near-death studies. A natural and gifted intuitive, Dr. Childs blends her clinical skills with the wisdom traditions of the world to offer a unique voice to those seeking deeper answers to life's quandaries.

A self-taught wordsmith who writes from the heart, her style is rich with metaphor and symbolism. Her debut title, ***Will You Dance?***, was the recipient of three national literary awards after its publication in 2002. Her second book, ***Halfway Across the River***, won the 2008 Benjamin Franklin Gold Medal and the 2009 Silver Nautilus Award. A gifted speaker, she travels extensively sharing her unique and inspired message with audiences throughout the United States and abroad.

Dr. Childs spends her days living between doorways. Many days find her standing in the doorway at life's end, as she assists the dying and their families to find peace and meaning in their journeys. Other days find her in the doorway of new beginnings as she takes her place next to her husband Brian, in a bustling family infused with the energy of three young lives that are newly unfolding. For her, it is the perfect balance of two worlds: the quiet wisdom of life's end, and the symphony of life emerging.

She lives in the western United States with her husband, and their three children.

Contact her at: www.onecandle.net

About the Artist

Ann Rothan

"Painting Sacred Art has been a slow unfolding inner experience since 1968. For years I kept paintings I called "visual meditations" hidden. There was a sense that if anyone saw them they would see my soul, which would then be open to scrutiny. Since my spirituality is deeply personal, this caused a major conflict. My transition came when others, sincerely moved by the art, saw a "portal of entry" for their meditation. As people began commissioning me to paint their "visual meditations," a strong desire to complete a body of work about spirituality, using veils of color, movement and symbolism began.

I see the Sacred Artist as the vision keeper, preparing the planet for what will be a deep spiritual awakening. "AS ABOVE, SO BELOW." To bring the higher consciousness into the earthly plane through symbols, color, form and subject is the work of the Sacred Artists."

"I see the Sacred Artist as the vision keeper..."

www.whereangelsdwell.com

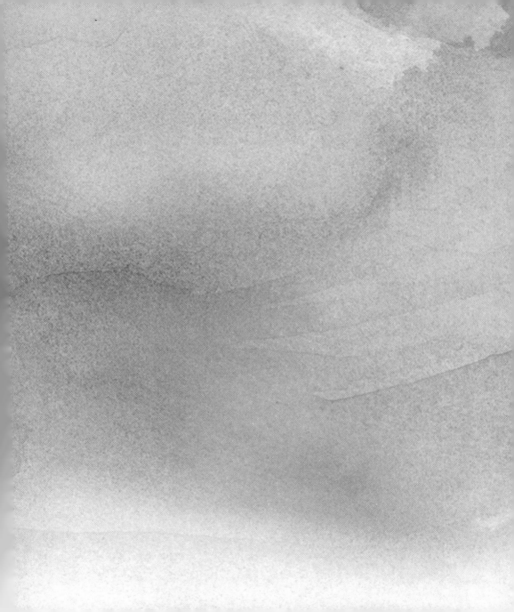